# ONCE UPON A RAINBOW

Nancy Faber

Colorful solos which develop

musical expression and creativity at the piano

Production: Frank and Gail Hackinson
Production Coordinator: Marilyn Cole
Editors: Victoria McArthur and Edwin McLean
Cover and Illustrations: Terpstra Design, San Francisco
Engraving: GrayBear Music Company, Hollywood, Florida

FABER
PIANO ADVENTURES®

ISBN 978-1-61677-103-4

A Note to the Teacher

Once Upon a Rainbow **Book One** is the first collection in a three-book series dedicated to color and fantasy at the piano. The theme of rainbows appears in a variety of musical settings with captivating lyrics to spark the imagination of the student.

Book One is written for the early elementary piano student. The focus on tone color and interpretation fosters musical growth while developing early reading skills. Rests are minimally used to increase student awareness of melodic shape and forward rhythmic motion.

Short creative opportunities that "spin" from the pieces help to inspire the student's composing talent.

As each piece is learned, the student may wish to color a new part of the rainbow located on the inside back cover of the book. (The 7 pieces complete the 7 colors of the rainbow.)

Enjoy this early-level exploration of musical color at the piano!

CONTENTS

1. A Rainbow is a Smile
(Turned Upside Down)

Words by Crystal Bowman

E - ven though it's rain - ing I'll not frown, for a rain - bow is a smile turned up - side down. Right side up or up - side down, a

Teacher Duet: (Student plays **1 octave higher**)

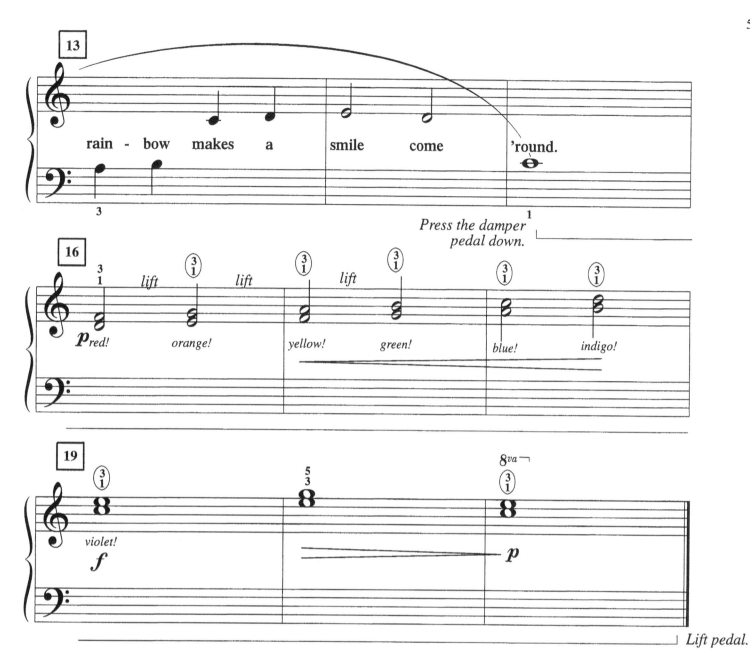

Optional: After learning this piece, turn to the inside back cover and color the "red" area on the rainbow.

CREATING AT THE PIANO: What interval does the right hand play from measure 16 to the end?

2nd or **3rd** (circle one)

Create "rainbow colors" by playing six different 3rds high on the piano.
Play slowly, holding the damper pedal down. Listen to the colors blend!

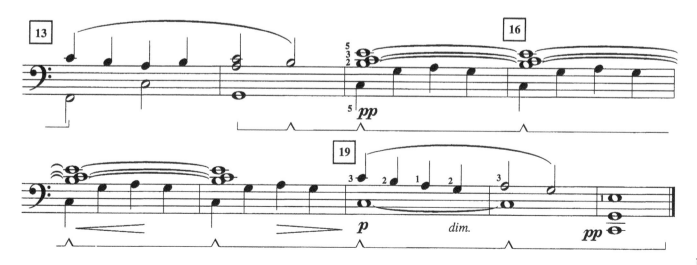

2. Most of All I Like Rainbows

Words by Crystal Bowman
Quick and playful (♩ = 100-112)

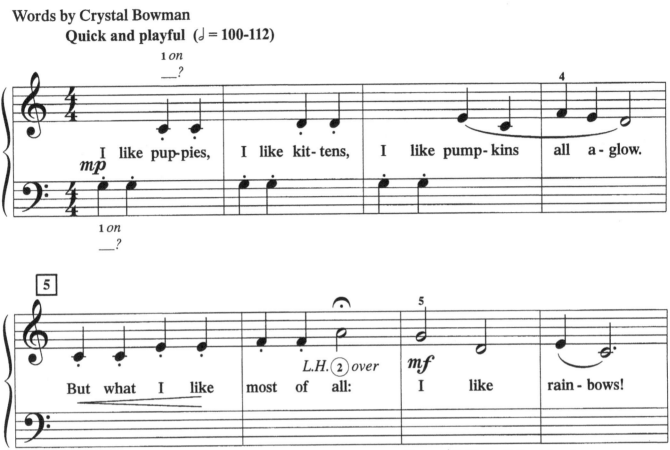

I like pup-pies, I like kit-tens, I like pump-kins all a-glow.

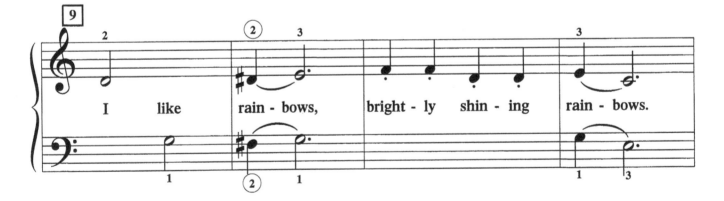

But what I like most of all: I like rain-bows!

(Return L.H. to C Position.)

I like rain-bows, bright-ly shin-ing rain-bows.

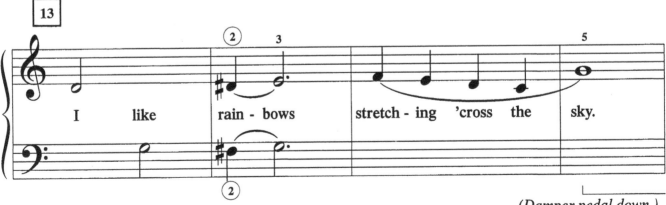

I like rain-bows stretch-ing 'cross the sky.

(Damper pedal down.)

Optional: After learning this piece, turn to the inside back cover and color the "orange" area on the rainbow.

CREATING AT THE PIANO: Create "raindrops" at the piano by playing high keys with a *staccato* touch. Make the raindrops fall gradually faster, then slow down and stop. You may use the damper pedal as you play.

3. A Double Rainbow

Words by Crystal Bowman

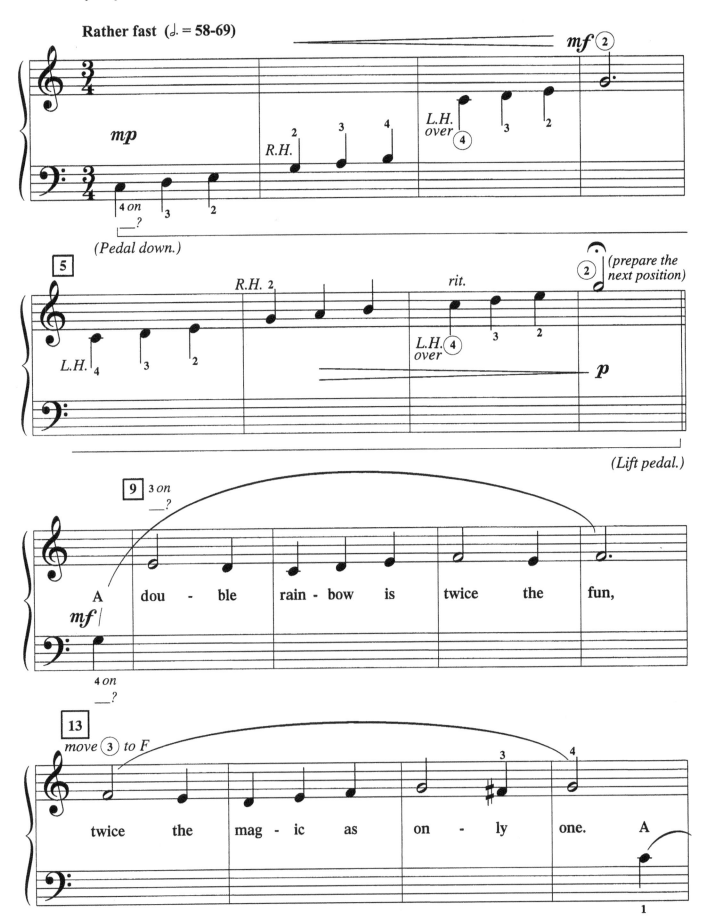

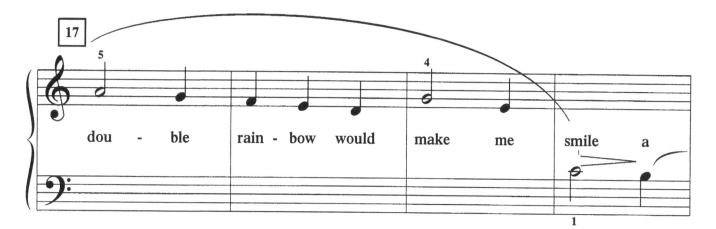

dou - ble   rain - bow   would   make   me   smile   a

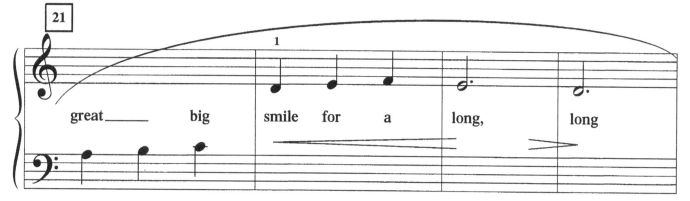

great_____   big   smile   for   a   long,   long

(Pedal down.)

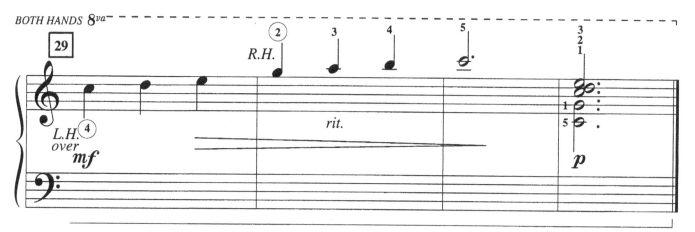

BOTH HANDS 8va

Optional: After learning this piece, turn to the inside back cover and color the "yellow" area on the rainbow.

CREATING AT THE PIANO: Hold the damper pedal down and create a "double rainbow." Play C-E-G (R.H. 1-3-5) *forte*, then repeat the pattern one octave higher playing *piano*.

Can you create a rainbow pattern of your own, then repeat it one octave higher?

4. I'm a Walking Rainbow

Words by Jennifer MacLean

Fast march, "in two" ($\dot{\,}$ = 100-112)

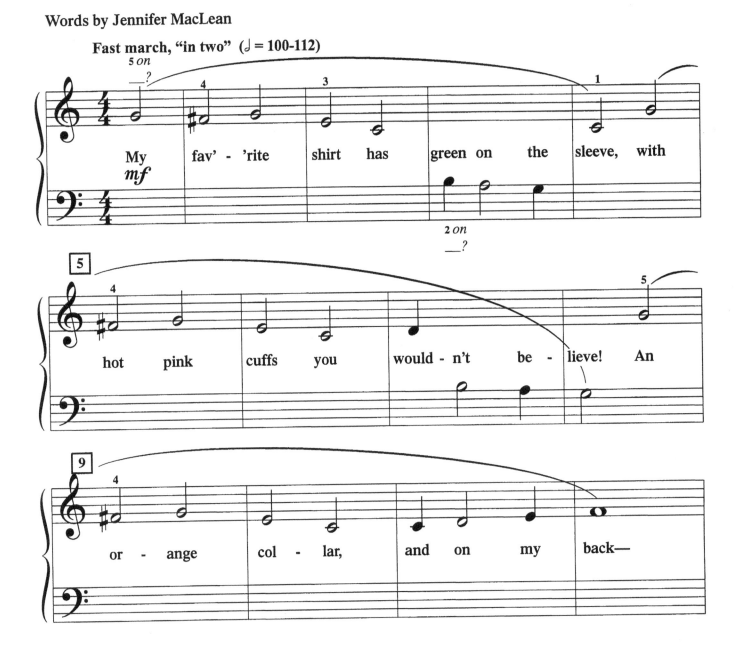

My fav' - 'rite shirt has green on the sleeve, with

hot pink cuffs you would - n't be - lieve! An

or - ange col - lar, and on my back—

Teacher Duet: (Student plays **1 octave higher**)

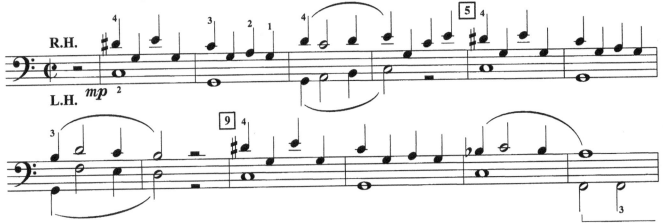

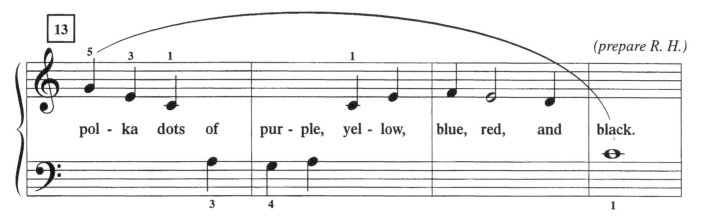

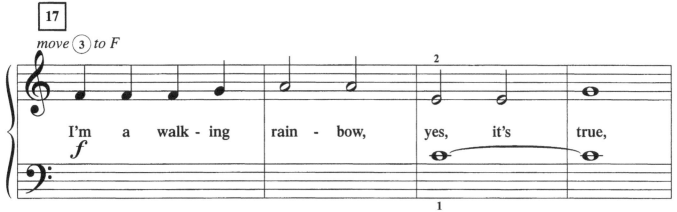

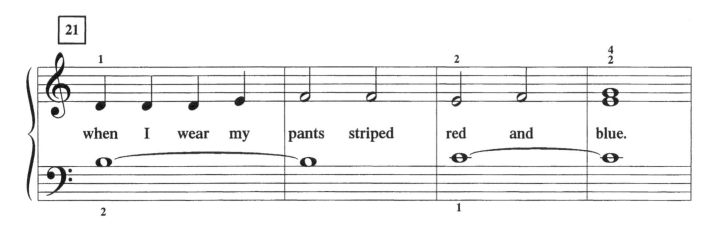

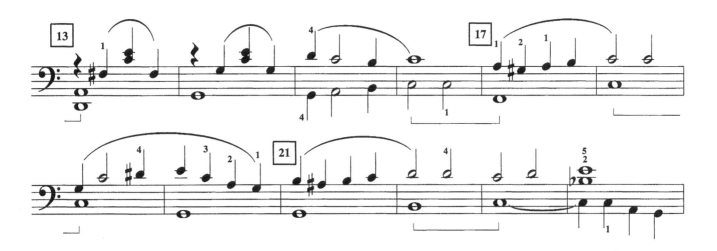

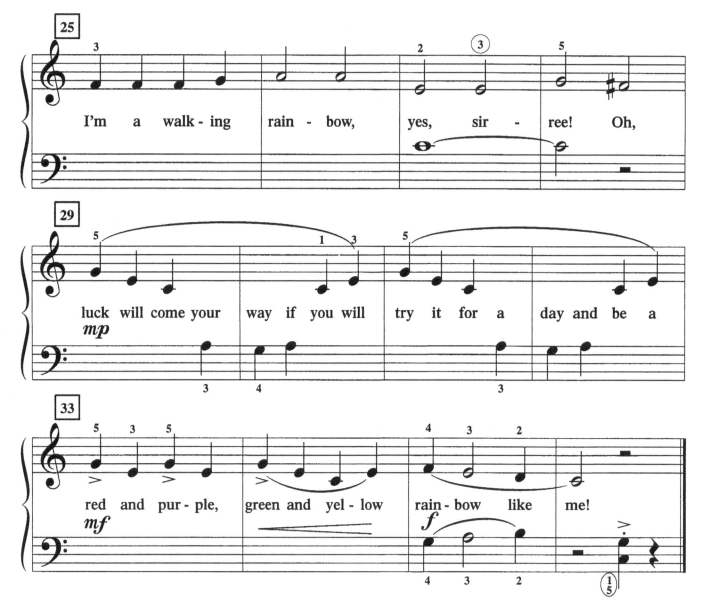

Lyrics (measures 25–36):

I'm a walk-ing rain - bow, yes, sir - ree! Oh,

luck will come your way if you will try it for a day and be a

red and pur - ple, green and yel - low rain - bow like me!

Optional: After learning this piece, turn to the inside back cover and color the "green" area on the rainbow.

CREATING AT THE PIANO: Imagine that the sound of each note below is a color in the rainbow. Play, *listen*, and connect each note to the color you think fits the best. (There is no wrong answer.)

yellow red blue green

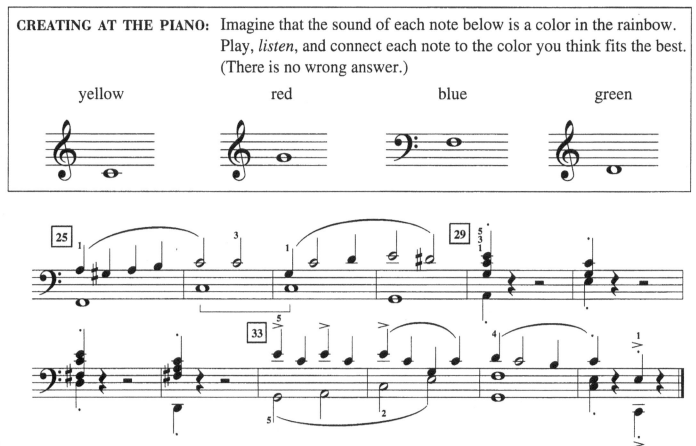

5. Rainbow, Rainbow

Words by Crystal Bowman

Rather quickly (♩ = 72-84)

Optional: After learning this piece, turn to the inside back cover and color the "blue" area on the rainbow.

Note to Teacher: This piece should be taught to the student by rote, line by line over several lessons.
(The benefits of learning a piece by rote include: use of the full keyboard range, development of aural memory, and recognition of musical patterns.)

Dear student: The music here is mainly for your teacher. Listen carefully as your teacher plays. Following the words, rhythm, and keyboards will help you to learn the piece.

6. The Storm and the Rainbow

Hold the damper pedal down for the entire piece.

b - e - c - o - m - e   l - o - u - d - e - r

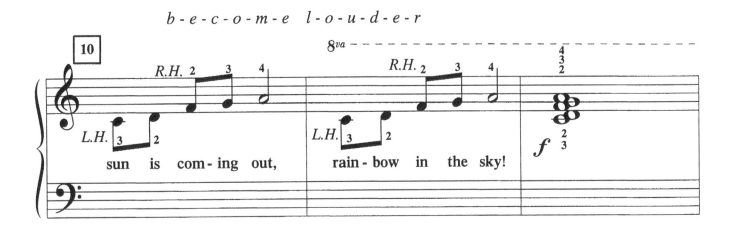

10

R.H. 2 — 3 — 4

sun   is   com - ing   out,

L.H. 3 — 2

8va

R.H. 2 — 3 — 4

rain - bow   in   the   sky!

4
3
2

𝆑   2
3

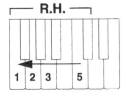

R.H.

1 2 3   5

S - l - o - w - i - n - g   d - o - w - n

13   (*still 8va*)

5 — 3 — 2 — 1   5 — 3 — 2 — 1   5 — 3 — 2 — 1   5 — 3 — 2 — 1

mp

Rain   is   stop-ping,   rain   is   stop-ping.   rain   is   stop-ping,   rain   is   stop-ping.

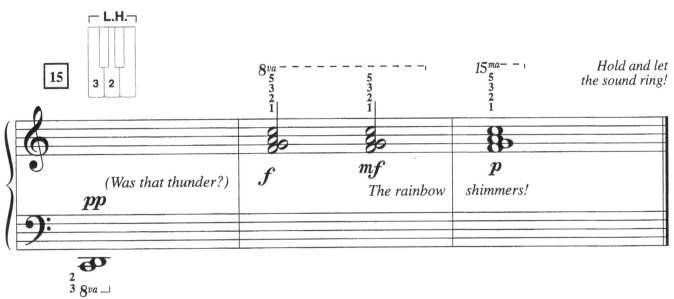

L.H.

3 2

15

8va
5
3
2
1

15ma
5
3
2
1

*Hold and let
the sound ring!*

(*Was that thunder?*)   𝆑   *mf*   *p*

pp   *The rainbow*   *shimmers!*

2
3   *8va*

Optional: After learning this piece, turn to the inside back cover and color the "indigo" (dark blue) area on the rainbow.

CREATING AT THE PIANO: Your teacher may ask you to make up your own version of
The Storm and the Rainbow using the black keys.

FF1103

7. At the End of the Rainbow

Words by Crystal Bowman

Gently moving (♩ = 144-160)

At the end of the rain - bow there's mag - ic, I'm told.

At the end of the rain - bow's a big pot of gold.

Teacher Duet: (Student plays **1 octave higher**)

poco cresc.

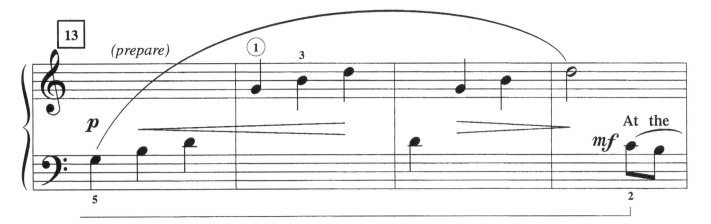

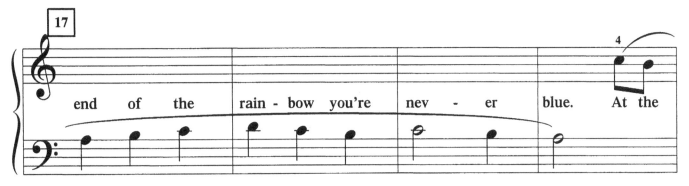

18

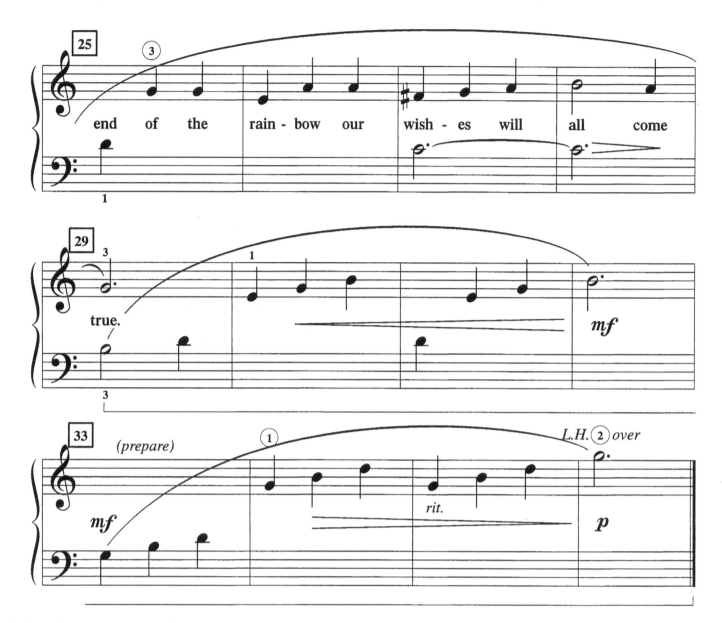

end of the rain - bow our wish - es will all come

true.

mf

(prepare) *mf* *rit.* *p* L.H. ② over

Optional: After learning this piece, turn to the inside back cover and color the "violet" (light purple) area on the rainbow.

CREATING AT THE PIANO: Can you play the pattern used in the last 4 measures with both hands beginning on E? Beginning on C? Beginning on A? (Use only white keys.)

Your Original Rainbow Solo (an optional composing project)

You have been exploring "rainbow sounds" as you learned the pieces in this book.
Now you may enjoy composing your own rainbow piece!

Your teacher will help you write the notes and rhythm on the staffs below,
or you may record it on a cassette tape.

_____

(title of your piece)

Music Dictionary

After finishing the book, can you correctly pronounce and define these musical terms for your teacher?

Dynamic Signs: "Dynamics" refers to the loudness and softness of the music.

pp	p	mp	mf	f
pianissimo	*piano*	*mezzo-piano*	*mezzo-forte*	*forte*
very soft	soft	medium soft	medium loud	loud

crescendo
get louder

diminuendo
get softer

SIGN	TERM	DEFINITION
>	**accent**	Play this note louder.
	a tempo	Return to the original tempo (speed).
⌢	*fermata*	Hold this note longer than usual.
♭	**flat**	Lower the note a half step (the nearest key to the left).
	interval	The distance between two pitches. (Ex., C to D is a 2nd; C to E is a 3rd.)
	legato	Play smooth and connected, with no break in the sound.
♮	**natural**	Cancels a sharp or flat; a natural is always a white key.
└─────┘	**pedal marking**	Depress the damper pedal (right foot pedal) after you play the note or chord; release at the end of the pedal mark.
	phrase	A musical idea or thought. Think of a phrase as a "musical sentence." A phrase is often shown in the music with a slur, also called a *phrase mark*.
rit.	*ritardando*	Gradually slow down the tempo.
⌒	**slur**	A curved line over or under a group of notes. It means to play legato (connected).
♯	**sharp**	Raise the note a half step (the nearest key to the right).
•	*staccato*	Lift off the key to create a crisp, detached sound.
⌒	**tie**	Play the note *once*, but hold for the length of both notes combined.
	8va	Play one octave higher. Written below the bass staff, it means to play one octave lower. (from Italian *ottava*)
	15ma	Play two octaves higher. (from Italian *quindicesima*)